GREAT
BIBLE
STORIES

GREAT
BIBLE
STORIES

Told by Ben Alex
Illustrated by Jose Perez Montero

scandinavia

Great Bible Stories

Published by Scandinavia Publishing House 2009
Scandinavia Publishing House
Drejervej 15,3 DK-2400 Copenhagen NV, Denmark
Tel. (45) 3531 0330 Fax (45) 3531 0334
E-mail: info@scanpublishing.dk
Web: www.scanpublishing.dk

Text copyright © Ben Alex
Illustrations copyright © Jose Perez Montero
Design by Ben Alex
Printed in China
Hardcover ISBN 978 87 7247 025 2
Softcover ISBN 978 87 7247 026 9

THE OLD TESTAMENT

Adam and Eve in the Garden of Eden

God created heaven and earth.

LET THERE BE LIGHT!

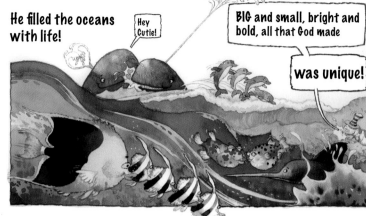

He filled the oceans with life!

Hey Cutie!

BIG and small, bright and bold, all that God made

was unique!

Next! Let's see...

My turn.

Elephants, kangaroos, and peacocks – just a few of my favorites.

God made Adam and Eve and put them in a lovely garden called Eden. He gave Adam the special job of naming the animals.

God had one command: "You may eat fruit from all the trees in the garden. But don't eat from the Tree of Knowledge."
One day a snake slithered up to Eve...

Come on, Eve! One bite won't hurt.

Okay.

God sent Adam and Eve out of the garden.

Bye, guys! We'll miss you.

Life was tough. Adam and Eve had to work hard. They also raised two sons.

Their sons Cain and Abel were different from each other

Some left-overs will be good enough.

My VERY best lamb for God.

Abel was a shepherd. He offered a lamb to God. Cain was a farmer. He offered God some grain.

Well, who do you think has the better attitude?

God accepted Abel's gift. Cain was so jealous he decided to kill his brother.

La-de-da!

Uh-oh

But God saw what Cain had done. He forced Cain to leave his home and become a wanderer.

Here comes that twerp now...

Noah and the Great Flood

People began to disobey God more and more. God wanted a new beginning. He decided to flood the earth and start again.

NOAH!

But there was one man God was pleased with.

Alligators, check! Snakes, check! Elephants, check!

God told Noah to build an ark and take onboard his family and a male and female of each kind of animal.

Yikes! I sure hope this ramp holds two elephants.

Rain flooded the earth for forty days and forty nights.

The flood was so great it covered the highest mountaintops.

When the rain finally stopped, Noah sent a dove out in search of land.

Land, ho!

Yow! I think I'm still seasick.

Y-i-p-p-e-e

Finally, the ark reached dry land. The animals bounded out and explored their new home.

I call this spot. Everyone got it?

You have been good to us, Lord!

Everyone was thankful to be on dry land. Noah gave God an offering.

But God had an even bigger surprise...

God gave the people a beautiful gift. He put a rainbow in the sky.

The Lord has promised never to flood the earth again!

A rainbow is a sign of God's never-ending love.

5

The Tower of Babel

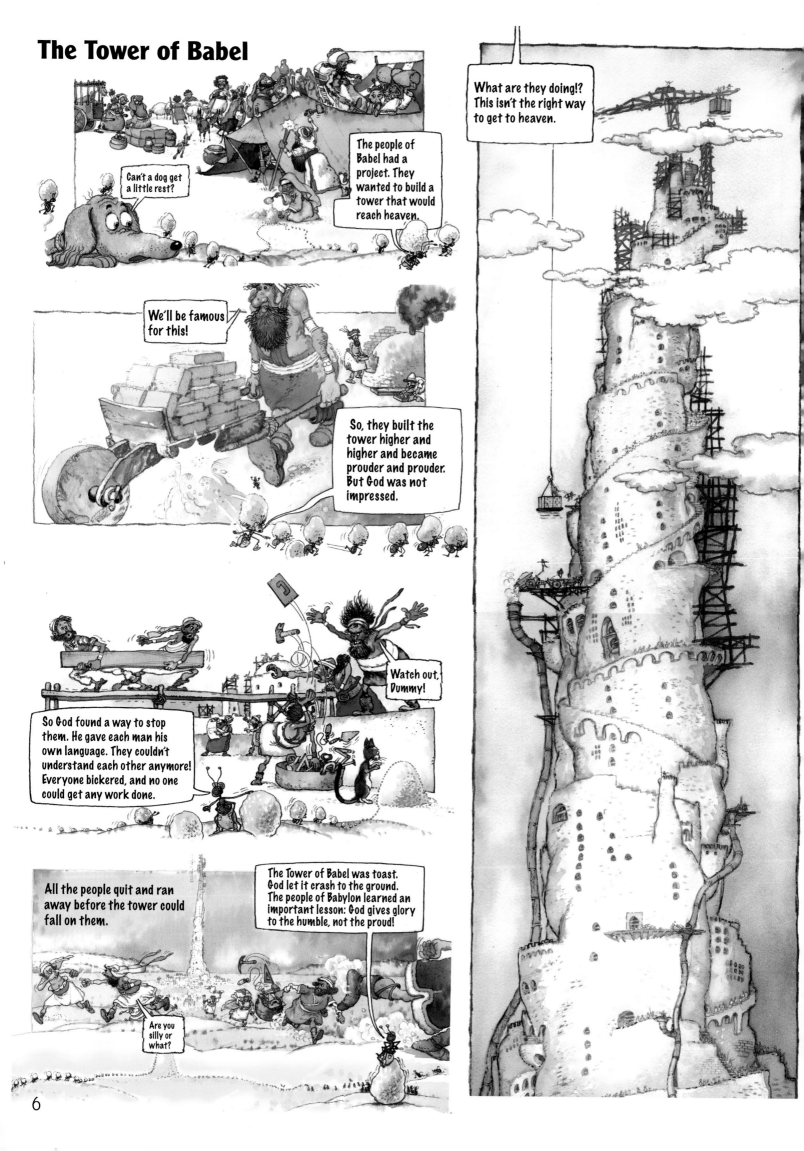

Can't a dog get a little rest?

The people of Babel had a project. They wanted to build a tower that would reach heaven.

We'll be famous for this!

So, they built the tower higher and higher and became prouder and prouder. But God was not impressed.

Watch out, Dummy!

So God found a way to stop them. He gave each man his own language. They couldn't understand each other anymore! Everyone bickered, and no one could get any work done.

All the people quit and ran away before the tower could fall on them.

Are you silly or what?

The Tower of Babel was toast. God let it crash to the ground. The people of Babylon learned an important lesson: God gives glory to the humble, not the proud!

What are they doing!? This isn't the right way to get to heaven.

Abraham's Sacrifice

Abraham was a servant of God.

He lived with his wife Sarah, their many servants and all their animals.

God sent Abraham on a journey.

Pack up! It's time to go to a new land.

Let's go, Sarah!

Huh? That little tortoise is beating me!

One night Abraham heard God's voice calling him.

Abraham, can you count the stars?

But there were too many to count. God told Abraham, "You will have as many descendants as there are stars in the sky!"

Years later, some travelers came by Abraham's tent. They promised him he would have a child with his wife Sarah.

Ha-ha

God hasn't forgotten His promise. Sarah is soon going to give birth to a baby boy.

But Sarah didn't believe it. She thought she was far too old to have any children.

God kept His promise. Sarah gave birth to baby Isaac. Isaac was a giggling, happy baby. Abraham adored him.

Thank you, God, for giving Isaac to us!

God wanted to test Abraham's obedience. He asked him to kill Isaac on an alter.

Little Isaac could not see what was about to happen. He obeyed his father, just as Abraham obeyed his father.

What are we sacrificing, Dad?

God will provide, Son.

Just as Abraham lifted his dagger, an angel stopped him! Abraham dropped his knife. "You have proved your love for God by nearly giving up your son. That is enough."

Whew! That was a close one. God never turns his back on the people that trust in Him.

STOP!!

Abraham squeezed Isaac tight. He never wanted to let go.

God blessed Abraham and Isaac. He made their descendants outnumber the stars, and they blessed every nation.

I love you, Son!

Joseph and His Jealous Brothers

Jacob loved Joseph more than any of his other sons.

Joseph, I bought this fancy coat for you.

Look at that little twerp! Who does he think he is? Some kind of prince?

Joseph's brothers threw him into a pit.

Let's get rid of him!

Meanwhile, some traveling traders came toward them.

Joseph's brothers sold him to the traders. They took him to Egypt and sold him as a slave.

Joseph worked as a servant for Potiphar, the king's official.

But one day Potiphar got angry at Joseph and threw him in prison. His cellmates were having strange dreams. "Tell me about them, and I'll tell you what they mean," Joseph said. So they told him.

Amazing! Joseph can interpret dreams!

The king heard about Joseph's gift for interpreting dreams. He called for him.

Tell me the meaning of my dream!

"Seven scrawny cows came up out of the sea. They gobbled up seven fat cows." Joseph told the king, "Your dream means seven years of famine are coming. You need a wise man to be in charge."

The king told Joseph, "You're wise. I'll make you my governor."

Back in Canaan, Joseph's brothers were hungry. They journeyed to Egypt to buy grain. They had no idea Joseph was the governor.

Joseph forgave his brothers. "Stay in Egypt," he told them, "and I will take care of you!" And that's exactly what they did.

Moses Rescues God's People

One day the princess of Egypt saw a baby in a basket floating on the river.

He's cute! I'll take him to the palace and call him Moses.

Moses grew up in the palace, but he never forgot his people, the Hebrews. They were forced to be slaves for the Egyptians.

One day Moses saw a burning bush in the desert. Suddenly a voice spoke aloud.

My people are slaves. But I've chosen you to free them!

Holy smokes! God is speakin' from a bush!

As the Israelites journeyed, God came down and met Moses on Mount Sinai. He gave Moses the Ten Commandments.

The Ten Commandments were to help God's people know how to live right.

After 40 years of wandering, the Israelites finally had a new home. But Moses was old, and it was time for him to be with God.

Go and take the land that God has given you!

God led the people to the Promised Land. It was lush and green and full of ripe fruit.

The Hebrews packed up their things and followed Moses out of Egypt. When they came to the sea, Moses lifted his walking stick. God parted the waters and the people crossed over.

The people were free! When the Egyptians tried to chase them, the waves swallowed them up.

Joshua and the Battle of Jericho

Before they entered the Promised Land, Moses chose his helper Joshua to lead the people.

God is with you, Joshua!

God promised to be with Joshua. "Trust in me, and there will be no reason to be afraid," God said.

Joshua found out there were enemies in the land. He led his army toward the city of Jericho.

How are we going to beat them, Joshua?

Joshua's army was small, and the city of Jericho was big.

But Joshua told his army, "Have courage—God is with us!"

The people set up camp outside Jericho and prepared for battle.

Some men brought spears, but they didn't need them.

God told the people to march around Jericho for six days.

God is going to work a miracle!

On the seventh day, God told them to circle around the city seven times. This time he told them to blow their trumpets.

Toot, toot! Joshua fought the battle of Jericho, Jericho, Jericho...

On the seventh time around, the army shouted and sang out praises.

...and the walls came tumbling down!

Go take the city!

God kept his promise. Joshua and the Israelites didn't win the battle because they were tough warriors; they won because they had faith in God!

Gideon and His Brave Soldiers

Over time the Hebrews began to forget God. The Midianites came along and began to bully them.

They stole their crops and burned down their houses. The Hebrews were miserable.

God, DO something!

Where's God?

Sigh

Gideon, God has chosen you to save your people!

Me? I'm just an ordinary guy.

One day a man named Gideon was visited by an angel.

"God will help you!" said the angel. "But you must believe in Him with your whole heart."

God told Gideon to tear down Baal's altar. "We'll build a new altar," Gideon told his friends, "and this time we'll make one for the Lord God and worship Him alone."

GONK!

WHAMMMMM!

Take that!

Crash! Klink! Pow! Gideon and his friends tore down the false idols.

Gideon prepared the people for battle against the Midianites. "God is with us. Don't be afraid!" he told them.

Count me in, Gideon!

Then God said to Gideon,

"Your army is too big. I'll help you win with fewer men."

"Take your men down to the water," God said. "Watch how they drink the water. Send home the ones who kneel down. But take all the ones who lap up the water like dogs."

Ready to fight? You're in!

God wanted to show Gideon that victory was about faith, not numbers.

Gideon gave each man a torch and a trumpet. The soldiers sneaked up on the enemy camp and blasted their instruments.

What's that?

An attack! Where's my sword?

HUH?!

The Midianites panicked! They scrambled over one another trying to run away. God let Gideon win with only 300 men!

11

Samson in Trouble

God had given Samson a special power. His long hair gave him strength. As long as his hair was never cut, his strength grew and grew.

Samson was strong and tough, even as a kid.

Samson got it again!

Oops!?

Samson grew up, and his strength doubled.

Nothing was too tough for Samson!

One day while Samson was traveling, he heard a noise...

Huh?

You don't scare ME!

SLAAMMMMMM

ARGH

Roaaar! A lion popped out of the underbrush! Samson threw him off with his bare hands.

Samson was angry at the Philistines. He lit some foxes tails on fire and let them run through their fields.

The fields burned, and the Philistines were furious.

SNAP

The Philistines caught Samson and tied him up. But that wasn't enough to keep Samson down.

He snapped off those ropes lik burnt cloth an ran away.

The Philistines paid Samson's girlfriend Delilah to find out what made him strong.

Cut it—before he wakes up!

Delilah found out that Samson's hair made him strong.

So the Philistines came and cut it off while Samson was asleep in Delilah's lap.

Samson was taken captive by the Philistines. They poked out his eyes and took turns making fun of him. But time went by, and Samson's hair started to grow back...

God, give me strength for one last feat. Let me pull down this temple and crush my enemies.

God answere his prayers!

Ruth Marries Boaz

Once there was an old woman named Naomi. She had a husband and two sons. Both of her sons married. One of the women was named Ruth.

When Naomi's husband and sons died, Ruth promised to stay with her, no matter what.

At that time there was a famine in the land. People were starving. Naomi and Ruth packed up all their things and left to find food.

Naomi tried to tell Ruth to go back to her own family. But Ruth stuck with Naomi.

Where you go, I will go.

Finally the two women reached Bethlehem. Naomi had relatives there, and she hoped to find help.

Home, sweet home!

The two women were hungry. Ruth promised to go find food as soon as they arrived.

Boaz was Naomi's relative. He let Ruth pick up the leftover wheat in his field.

"Boaz let you have all this?" Naomi asked. "Bless him!"

Every day Ruth collected wheat. She was never turned away.

Take as much as you like!

One day Naomi told Ruth, "Why don't you lie down at Boaz's feet tonight?"

If a woman lay down at a man's feet, it meant she would like to be his wife.

Boaz and Ruth were married.

I love you, Ruth!

God has been good to me.

Here comes the bride! Hear comes the groom! Here come the birds singing, while the flowers bloom!

Boaz and Ruth were blessed with a son. They named him Obed.

Hey, Kiddo!

Zippity-do! Who knew?! Little Obed would grow up to be the grandfather of King David!

13

The Shepherd Boy Who Became King

Solomon the Wise King

David had a son named Solomon. After his father died, Solomon became king.

One night, God spoke to him in a dream.

Tell me what you want, and I will give it to you.

Solomon asked for wisdom. So God made him the wisest king that ever lived.

One day two women came to Solomon.

Help! This woman wants to take my baby!

She's a liar—the baby is mine!

Cut the baby in half. Then you can both have him!

No Sir, give her the baby. Just don't kill him!

Solomon knew that the real mother was the one who cared about the child. He gave the baby back to her.

Solomon wanted to build a temple for God, but he needed wood. He wrote his friend, the king of Tyre, for supplies.

The king of Tyre sent pine and cedar logs. He also sent a load of workers to help build the temple.

For seven years Solomon oversaw the building of his temple. He wanted everything to be perfect. After all, it was God's house.

God told Solomon, "Be faithful and obey my words, and I promise to be with my people forever!" At last the temple was finished.

Word spread about Solomon's rich kingdom. The Queen of Sheba traveled all the way from Egypt just to see it for herself.

Solomon had everything —children, wives, riches, wisdom and power.

He was also a great poet, and he taught his children to love God.

God gave Solomon much more than he had asked for.

Elijah and the Prophets of Baal

Elijah was God's prophet. God was not pleased with the way his people were worshiping false gods. So Elijah went to the king with a warning.

It will not rain for a long time because you have disobeyed God!

King Ahab was furious with Elijah. He immediately banished him from the kingdom.

Elijah lived in the wild. God sent ravens to bring him food. But Elijah was still hungry so he asked a poor widow for some bread.

I don't have enough oil to feed us all.

Elijah told the woman to trust in God. So the woman used up all her oil. But God refilled her jar, and she never ran out again.

Elijah went back to the king and challenged him...

Let's see whose God is the true God! We will both build an altar and ask our god to set it on fire!

Ahab and his men prayed to their god. But nothing happened.

Hear us, great Baal!

Then it was Elijah's turn.

Lord, show these people you are the true God.

KA-BOOM!

At once, the wood caught on fire. King Ahab and his men were amazed.

Quick, go home! God is sending a rainstorm.

Finally God let the rain pour down again. The king jumped into his chariot and sped home. But even though Elijah had to run, he beat the king back to the city.

King Ahab still wanted to kill Elijah. Once again, he had to hide in the wild. He felt lonely, but he was not alone. God promised to be with him.

I can feel God move in the gentle breeze!

WOOOOSHH

God was not in the noise. He was not in the earthquake, nor in the fire...

Elijah was getting old. One day he went for a walk with his young friend Elisha. "It's time to say goodbye," Elijah told his friend. Just then, a light flashed in the sky! It was a flaming chariot, driven by horses. Elisha watched as the chariot diappeared.

Nothin' like a fiery chariot to getcha around!

Elijah went to be with God. Now it was Elisha's turn to be God's prophet.

Esther Saves Her People

The king was searching for a queen. He wanted the loveliest woman in the kingdom to be his bride.

Search is over, girls! Esther is the fairest of them all.

Hello, Esther!

But Esther was Jewish. She kept it a secret from the Persian king. The only person who knew her secret was her cousin Mordecai.

Mordecai came to visit Esther everyday.

The king married Esther. She became the queen with all the riches she desired.

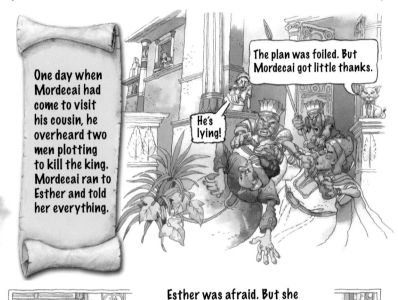

One day when Mordecai had come to visit his cousin, he overheard two men plotting to kill the king. Mordecai ran to Esther and told her everything.

He's lying!

The plan was foiled. But Mordecai got little thanks.

Haman, the king's special advisor, didn't like Mordecai because Mordecai wouldn't bow to him. So Haman ordered all Jews to be killed.

Oh God, have mercy on your people!

The people of Israel were devastated! They cried and called out to God. Mordecai had an idea. He went to Esther and told her what to do.

Esther was afraid. But she went to the king and begged him to save her people.

This was a very brave thing to do. Esther confessed to being Jewish even though it could've cost her life!

The king listened to Esther. He made a new law to honor Esther's people, the Jews.

No Jews shall be killed, and Mordecai will be the new advisor!

Praise God!

Esther and Mordecai were heroes! Everyone cheered for them.

The people all got together and celebrated with a big feast. God had come to the rescue of his people!

The Jewish people still celebrate the Feast of Purim to this day! Hey mouse, pass those fish sticks over this way!

Daniel Tells the King His Dream

The people of Israel worked as slaves in Babylon.

But a Jewish boy named Daniel was chosen by King Nebuchadnezzar to live in the palace.

Here are two great heroes of Babylon.

Funny hats!

Three of Daniel's friends were chosen, too. The boys had to learn a new language and a new way to dress and behave.

There was a lot to learn! The king even made the boys change their names.

But Daniel and his friends didn't forget about God. While the others bowed down to a statue, they prayed to the Lord God.

Oh, god of gold!

God, we will only worship you!

Hey good-lookin'!

Just give us water and vegetables.

I bet in ten days we'll be just as healthy and strong as all the others!

And while the others ate greedily, Daniel and his friends only ate the food that God approved.

Don't you see? God keeps us strong!

Just as Daniel had said, God did not let the lack of food affect them. They were just as healthy as the others and grew taller everyday.

Many years later, the king was giving a party. But something strange happened—he saw a hand writing on the wall!

What could it mean? He offered a reward to anyone who could read the writing.

Daniel told the king the writing meant his land would be taken. And soon the king's land was taken.

Daniel was right. Darius took over and became the new king. He refused to let Daniel pray to God.

King Darius had Daniel tied up and led away...

A little faith goes a long way! God never leaves His people.

Daniel was left for dead in a pit of hungry lions. So Daniel prayed to God. The Lord made those lions as tame as kittens.

The next day the king let Daniel go. He saw that Daniel's God was the true Lord.

God Sends Jonah to the City of Nineveh

God told a man named Jonah to go to the city of Nineveh with His message. But Jonah didn't want to. He hopped on a ship and hoped that God would not find him.

I'm out of here!

I don't know about you, but I have a feeling that's not such a good idea.

But while Jonah was onboard, God sent a terrible storm.

Why is this happening? Whose fault is it?

The captain and crew started to shake with fear. They woke Jonah up where he was sleeping.

"Surely it's my fault," Jonah cried. "God is punishing me. Throw me overboard!"

I can't swim!

So the crew threw Jonah into the raging sea. Jonah couldn't swim, and he began to sink deeper and deeper...

A huge whale swallowed Jonah. Inside the whale's stomach, Jonah prayed to God. Finally, God made the whale spit Jonah out again.

This time Jonah listened to God. He went back to speak God's word to the sinful people in Nineveh.

Now go, and tell people in Nineveh about me!

People of Nineveh, listen! God is very angry with you! He will destroy this city in 40 days!

The people of Nineveh listened to Jonah. Even the king took off his robe and sat in the dirt to show his obedience.

Turn back to God!

May He have mercy!

The people hoped that God would change his mind. They stopped sinning and began to follow the Lord's ways.

Jonah was certain that God would destroy Nineveh. He found a shady spot to watch the action. But nothing happened. God decided to spare the city.

Jonah, why are you angry?

Didn't I spare the city?

I thought you were going to destroy it! Now I look like a fool!

Jonah was mad. Nothing could satisfy him. But soon his anger wore him out, and he fell asleep.

I'm so angry I could die!

God let a worm eat all the leaves from the tree Jonah was sleeping under. The scorching sun burned Jonah's skin. He got even more irritated.

God told him, "You are angry because of a tree. But I made the tree and cared for it—just like I care for the people of Nineveh." Jonah finally learned his lesson.

THE NEW TESTAMENT

The Birth of Jesus

A long time ago, there was a woman named Mary. One night Mary woke up and saw an angel by her bed.

Yes?

"Good news! You're going to give birth to the Son of God!"

Later, an angel visited Mary's husband-to-be Joseph.

Mary is pregnant. Take her as your wife. Her child is from God!

Joseph trusted the angel and took Mary as his wife.

Mary and Joseph had to travel to Bethlehem to be counted and taxed. The city was crammed full of people, and there was no place to sleep.

Sorry. No room.

Oh, no! Mary was almost ready to give birth!

Look, Mary, a stable! That's where we'll stay for the night.

It was a sh for animal

There Mary gave birth to her baby boy. The angel told her to name him Jesus.

Where is he?

There he is in Mary's arms!

Angels sang out, "Peace on earth and good will towards men!"

Word spread that a child of God had been born. The shepherds left their fields and came running to see Jesus. They kneeled down and worshiped him.

Meanwhile far away, three wise men saw a bright star in the sky.

A king must be born!

They followed the star and finally came to Bethlehem.

The wise men came with gifts for baby Jesus!

Happy birthday, Jesus.

Gifts of gold, perfume and sweet oils were laid at Jesus' feet. The wise men told Mary, "We've traveled a long way to see the King of the Jews." It was a very special night for everyone.

Jesus Grows Up

In a dream God warned Joseph that King Herod was planning to kill all the baby boys of Bethlehem.

King Herod was jealous. He hoped his plan would get rid of the new King.

So Joseph fled under the cover of night with Mary and Jesus.

They stayed in Egypt until it was safe to come home. Then they returned to Nazarath and raised Jesus.

Once during Passover, Mary and Joseph lost Jesus in the crowded streets of Jerusalem. They searched everywhere.

Finally they found Jesus. "Where were you?" they cried.

Jesus answered, "I was in the temple! Didn't you know I would be in my Father's house?"

Jesus Calls Disciples

When Jesus was a grown man, he went to a wedding party. The guests had no more wine to drink.

Fill these jars with water!

As the jars were filled, the water turned into wine. The people were amazed!

Do you think anyone would notice if I went for a little dip in here?

Jesus began to teach people about God's Word.

Love those who hurt you.

Give to those in need.

Treat others with loving kindness,.

There you go, Sweetie.

Jesus gained followers. 12 of them became his disciples.

One of Jesus' disciples was Simon Peter. He was a fisherman.

Jesus told Simon Peter to become a fisher of men!

Dom-da-dum-da-dum

The 12 men left everything behind to follow Jesus.

Lookin' for a thirteenth disciple? Look no further!

Trust in me, John!

Jesus Teaches About the Kingdom of God

Here is another story. A man knocked on his neighbor's door and asked for some bread. The neighbor didn't turn him away. He gave him all that he had.

When we pray to God it's like knocking on a door. God opens it every time.

Come on in! I think I have a stash of cheddar cheese.

Listen to this! Three men worked in a vineyard. One worked all day; another worked four hours, and the last worked only one hour. But they were all paid the same amount.

God treats his followers the same way. He does not reward our efforts; he rewards our faith! Believe in him, and you will have eternal life.

Jesus Works Miracles and Heals People

Jesus had been preaching all morning to a group of 5,000 people. By the afternoon the people began to feel hungry. "How can we feed them all?" the disciples asked Jesus.

A boy stepped forward and said, "You can have my lunch, Jesus!"

Thank you, my friend!

Jesus took the five loaves and two fishes and broke them in half. The disciples cried out, "That's still not enough, Jesus!"

But Jesus told the disciples to pass around the food anyway.

The food went around until everyone had plenty. There was even enough food left over to fill twelve baskets. Now that's something to chew on!

When people realized Jesus could work miracles, he gained even more followers.

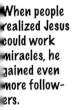

He healed the sick and cured the lepers. He made the blind see again. He never turned away anybody who trusted him.

Jesus healed me!

Please, help me!

One time a foreign woman came to Jesus. She had a sick daughter. The people grumbled, "She's not one of us. Why are you helping her?" Jesus replied, "Haven't I come to save the lost?" Then he healed her sick daughter.

How can Jesus heal like that?

It's the work of the devil!

Jesus healed me!

Many people were suspicious of Jesus. They thought he was just a trickster and a troublemaker.

This has gone too far. Jesus is claiming to be the Son of God! We'd better find a way to get rid of him.

That man is dangerous!

While Jesus was busy teaching his message of love, the priests were busy scheming against him. They kept a sharp eye on everything he did.

Jesus Tells Stories

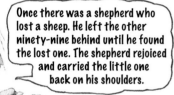

Once there was a shepherd who lost a sheep. He left the other ninety-nine behind until he found the lost one. The shepherd rejoiced and carried the little one back on his shoulders.

Jesus is the Good Shepherd. Each one of his sheep is important to him.

When a wolf comes, does the shepherd leave his sheep?

No buster! He protects them, just like Jesus protects us!

Grrr!

Get out of here!

Once there were two men who owed money. One owed a lot and the other owed a little. Neither of them had to pay it back. The man who owed a lot was the most thankful.

That's why sinners feel so grateful to Jesus!

Let me help you.

One time a man was robbed and left in a ditch. Two holy men walked on by. Finally a Samaritan came and helped the man.

Jesus wants us to be like the Good Samaritan. Help others!

You are the salt of the earth.

Salt gives flavor, but it also makes people thirsty! Jesus is the living water ready to quench our thirst.

Listen to me, and you'll be like the man who built his house on rock. It can stand firm against any storm!

Oh rats! I should have listened to that story, huh?

God's kingdom is here on earth! Such a wonderful treasure should never be let go.

The kingdom of Heaven is like a precious pearl. Those who love God will seek it out.

God doesn't sell his kingdom. It is priceless! He gives it to those who give up every-thing else to follow him.

The kingdom of God is invisible to the eye. But that doesn't mean it's not there. Plant the seeds of love and faith, and God's kingdom will grow!

When we listen and understand Jesus' words, we reap a big harvest.

Jesus Works More Miracles

Jesus was teaching in a crowded room. A crippled man could not get to Jesus, so his friends lowered him down through the roof.

Because of your friends' faith, you shall be well.

Jesus met another man who had been crippled for 38 years. "Pick up your mat and walk," Jesus told him. The man had faith and was healed.

Two blind men came to Jesus hoping he could heal them. Jesus put his hands over their eyes. Then he took his hands away. "You've healed us," they cried. "We can see!"

Jesus told the men, "You've been healed because of your faith. I am not the one who heals. It is God the Father who heals."

...can be ...led, too.

I trust you, Jesus. But all I see are shadows like trees.

Jesus put his hands over the man's eyes. When he took them away again, the blind man could see perfectly.

One time Jesus healed ten lepers.

Thank you, Jesus!

Only one came back to thank Jesus. "I healed ten men," Jesus said. "Yet you are the only one who has thanked me. Bless you!"

Jesus and His Friends

Jesus was known for his miracles far and wide. People began to wonder who he really was.

Who do people say I am?

One day Jesus gathered his friends and asked them a question.

Some say a prophet, others a great teacher...

Later, Jesus turned and asked them...

But you, who do YOU say that I am?

You are Christ the Lord!

"Bless you, Peter," Jesus replied. "God showed you the truth."

Jesus' good friend Lazarus died, so his sister Martha sent for Jesus.

Lazarus is ALIVE!

Jesus walked up to the tomb. "Lazarus, come out!" he called. At that moment, Lazarus came out wrapped in bandages. Jesus raised him to life!

One day Jesus took three of his friends up on a mountain. There they saw Jesus talking with the old prophets Moses and Elijah.

?

Jesus' clothes were bright white, and his face was shining like the sun! The disciples were convinced that Jesus was no ordinary man.

Jesus loved children. He said, "God's kingdom belongs to little ones such as these!"

"Unless you become like a child," Jesus said, "you cannot enter the kingdom of Heaven."

Stop fighting!

Jesus' disciples were arguing about who was the greatest among them.

Jesus told them, "The greatest one is not the one who is served. The greatest one is the one that serves others."

Some children were shooed away by Jesus' disciples. "He's busy," they told them.

Do you know what Jesus said? "Don't turn them away! Let the children come to me. They belong to God my Father."

Jesus told the people that they could learn a lot from children. "They trust in God with their whole hearts," he said.

Me next!

Jesus accepted everybody. People brought their children to Jesus, and he blessed every single one of them.

Jesus and his disciples were in a boat when a storm picked up.

Jesus, wake up; we're drowning!

Jesus stood up and stretched out his arms...

"Be still," he spoke. The waves and the wind obeyed. The disciples were speechless.

One time Jesus was praying on the shore. He saw his disciples out on the water caught in another storm.

Jesus walked out to them on top of the water. "It's a ghost!" they gasped. "No, it's me," Jesus said.

Come!

Let me walk out to you!

Peter wanted to be sure it was really Jesus. So he stepped out of the boat and walked toward him.

Peter looked down at his feet. He became nervous and cried, "I'm sinking!" Jesus reached for his hand. "Why don't you have faith in me? I won't let you fall."

29

Jesus Is Arrested and Killed

When Jesus visited Jerusalem, a big crowd came out to greet him.

Hosanna!

Everyone cheered and waved palm leaves. Jesus rode through the crowd on a donkey.

Jesus is King!

Judas, one of the disciples, plotted with the priests to have Jesus killed.

I can help you get Jesus arrested.

How?

Don't do it!

We'll pay!

Judas betrayed Jesus for 30 pieces of silver.

Meanwhile, Jesus ate the Last Supper with his disciples. He held up a glass of wine and broke a loaf of bread.

This wine is my blood. This bread is my body.

Soon I will leave you. It's time for me to return to my Father.

But before I do that, I must suffer.

Then Jesus told Judas, "Go and do what you have to do."

Please, pray with me.

Jesus knew what was going to happen. He felt scared and alone. He went to the Garden of Gethsemane to pray. But his disciples fell asleep.

Suddenly some soldiers came to arrest Jesus. Peter drew his sword and chopped off one of the soldiers' ears.

OUCHH!

STOP, Peter!

Jesus healed the man's ear and let them take him away.

Kill him!

What shall I do with Jesus?

Crucify him!

Jesus was taken to Pontius Pilate, the Roman governor.

The people who had once followed Jesus now turned their backs on him. They gathered outside Pilate's door as an angry mob.

Jesus had told Peter that he would deny him three times before the cock crowed. Peter did not believe him.

Cock-a-doodle-do

Sure enough, Peter denied Jesus three times after Jesus was arrested.

You're Jesus' disciple!

No I'm NOT.

NO

NO

Yes

Yes

Peter felt ashamed that he had denied Jesus. Later on, after Jesus had come back to life, Jesus forgave Peter.

It's OK, Peter. I know you love me.

Finally, we're rid of him!

Jesus was whipped and beaten. Then he had to carry his own cross up on a hill. He was crucified between two criminals and left to die.

Jesus Is Alive

Jesus' friends wrapped his body in clean cloth. They put him in an empty tomb and rolled a stone over the entry. Two soldiers stood guard on either side, making sure that no one stole the body and claimed Jesus was alive.

Two days later on Easter morning, they went back to visit the tomb. But the stone was rolled away.

Hello, anybody in there?

I have a feeling this bunch is about to hear some great news.

An angel appeared to them and said,

Jesus has risen! Jesus has risen!

YIPPPPEEE! This is the best Easter ever!

Is it true?

Can Jesus really be alive?

When the disciples got word, they raced to the tomb to see for themselves.

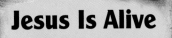

31

John waited outside while Peter searched the tomb. All he found were some bandages Jesus' was wrapped in. It was true!

?

Jesus promised his disciples he would rise three days after he was crucified. He had already left for Galilee.

Jesus appeared to all the disciples. But Thomas wouldn't believe until he touched Jesus' wounds.

Go ahead, Thomas. Touch the nail wounds in my hands.

But blessed are those that believe without seeing.

My Lord, it IS you!

One day when the disciples were fishing, they spotted Jesus on the shore. Peter jumped off the boat and swam toward him.

Come have some breakfast, Peter!

Peter was afraid Jesus would be angry. But Jesus had already forgiven Peter for denying him. "Do you love me, Peter?" Jesus asked. "Yes!" Peter answered, "Yes! Yes!"

Now I must go back to my Father in heaven. You must carry on what I started. Don't fear. I'll be with you always. God will send the Holy Spirit to you. He will teach you.

The Apostles Spread the Good News

Jesus may have gone back to God, but his Spirit was with the people. They did not forget his words. They knew that the kingdom of God belongs to those that believe in him. That is why it was so important for the disciples to spread Christ's message. They wanted the whole world to know about God's love. Just like Jesus, the disciples traveled and preached the word of God to all kinds of people.

Jesus was a miracle worker! Did I ever tell you about the time he walked on water? Well, you see—there was this storm...

One day the disciples were praying in a room. Suddenly a strong wind swept through the room.

The Holy Spirit was in the wind, and the disciples began to speak with confidence about God.

People gathered outside to see what was going on. Peter told them,

Jesus has died. But he rose again and lives on! He has sent us the Holy Spirit.

Believe in Jesus, and you will receive the Holy Spirit too!

One day Peter and John were walking to the temple when they saw a crippled man. "Can you spare a few coins?" the cripple man asked.

I've got something even better than money! Get up—you're healed in Jesus' name!

The man jumped for joy. The Holy Spirit healed him.

The leaders of Israel did not like the disciples. They thought the disciples were gaining too much power and preaching dangerous things. They arrested Peter and John.

That didn't keep Peter and John from speaking out about Jesus. "We won't keep quiet about our Lord," they said. To this day we can still read their words in the New Testament.

The disciple John also wrote one of the gospels. He wrote letters, too. And in Revelation we can read what John has to say about the return of Jesus, the King.

"The world is in darkness," John said, "because people don't know how to love one another. They only know how to steal and lie and cheat."

But when Jesus comes back, we will all be judged. We are God's children! When we love each other, we will bring light to a dark place.

Let your light shine! Play games, and enjoy God's world to show him your love.

Zzzz

But there was one man who did not care about Jesus' message. King Herod had many Christians arrested. Once again, Peter was thrown in jail.

An angel came and saved him while the guard was asleep.

Peter, get up! You're free.

Paul – Apostle to the World

Christians began to meet in private. If they spoke up about Jesus, they were arrested. So they had to encourage each other and strengthen their faith away from the prying eyes of King Herod.

A man named Saul worked for the Jewish leaders. He had Christians arrested.

Another Christian! Kill him!

One day a bright light shone in Saul's eyes and knocked him off his horse.

Saul, why are you against me?

I am Jesus—the one you are persecuting!

Huh?

Saul tried to get up, but he was blind.

Three days later, God gave Saul back his sight. He became a believer. He changed his name to Paul and began a new life of faith in Jesus.

?

Good morning, and God bless you!

Paul travelled all over the world to tell people about Jesus. Sometimes his friends Silas and Timothy came along.

"Don't let anyone look down on you because you are young," he told Timothy, "but be an example to others in love and faith!"

Eventually Paul and Silas were thrown in jail. But even then they sang out God's praises and shared his love with the other prisoners.

Praise God!

Paul was taken to Rome to be judged by the emperor.

The voyage across the sea took many days.

A huge storm came and rocked the ship. Paul saw that the captain and crew were afraid. Paul told them not to worry.

Don't worry. God will take care of us.

Paul urged his shipmates to trust in God. So he ordered his men to throw the cargo into the sea.

Let's jump off the ship before it sinks!

No, stay where you are if you don't want to drown.

This is gonna go bad. Anyone need an umbrella? Just a couple holes in it, that's all.

Finally the ship hit some rocks and broke apart.
"Get off the ship!" cried the captain. Everyone swam safely to shore.

They stayed on the island until winter had passed, and it was safe to go on.

At last, Paul arrived in Rome. He may have been a prisoner, but he was greeted like a hero. Christians came and cheered as Paul got off the ship.

God bless you all for coming out to greet me!

35

Jesus is God's gift to the world...

Paul was under house arrest, waiting for his trial. Meanwhile, people came and visited him. They liked to hear him preach.

While in prison, Paul wrote letters to friends, as well as churches.

Dear friends...

Paul encouraged believers to stay strong during rough times.

Heaven Ahead

In the last book of the Bible, the disciple John wrote about the glorious day when God will gather all believers in Jesus before his throne.

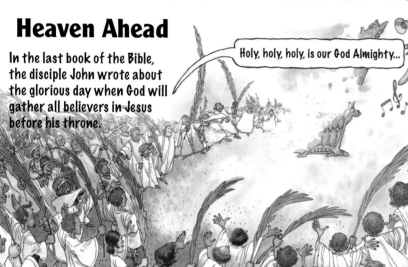

Holy, holy, holy, is our God Almighty...

John assures us that heaven will be a wonderful place. We will be close to God, and there will be no more sin!

Everyone's a winner h[...]

God will wipe every tear from our eyes. Everything will be made anew. We will worship the Lord with joy in our hearts.

We will love each other, and we will love ourselves too! We are a reflection of God. He has made us with his own hand. Heaven is a place to laugh and play—no more pain and no more tears!

Here's the truth: Anyone who does not accept God's kingdom like one of these children will never enter it.